I LOVE TO BRUSH MY TEETH
이를 닦는 것이 너무 좋아요

Shelley Admont
Illustrated by Sonal Goyal, Sumit Sakhuja

Copyright©2013 by S. A. Publishing
www.sachildrensbooks.com

All rights reserved. No part of this book may be reproduced in any form or by any electronic or mechanical means, including information storage and retrieval systems, without written permission from the publisher or author, except in the case of a reviewer, who may quote brief passages embodied in critical articles or in a review.

모든 권한을 보유합니다.

First edition, 2016
Translated from English by Ju Yeon Kang
한국어 번역가: 강주연

Library and Archives Canada Cataloguing in Publication
I Love to Brush My Teeth (Korean Bilingual Edition)/ Shelley Admont

ISBN: 978-1-77268-286-1 paperback
ISBN: 978-1-77268-285-4 eBook

Please note that the Korean and English versions of the story have been written to be as close as possible. However, in some cases they differ in order to accommodate nuances and fluidity of each language.

Although the author and the publisher have made every effort to ensure the accuracy and completeness of information contained in this book, we assume no responsibility for errors, inaccuracies, omission or any inconsistency herein.

for those I love the most
내가 가장 사랑하는 사람들에게

Clifton Park - Halfmoon Public Library
475 Moe Road
Clifton Park, New York 12065

Morning came and the sun was shining in the faraway forest. There, in a small house, lived little bunny Jimmy, with his parents and two older brothers.

머나먼 숲 속 나라에 해가 뜬 어느 날이었어요. 숲 속에 있는 작은 집에는 아기 토끼 지미와 부모님 그리고 두 형제가 살고 있었지요.

Mom came into the room that Jimmy shared with his brothers.

엄마가 지미와 지미의 형제들이 있는 방에 왔어요.

First she kissed the oldest brother, who slept peacefully in his blue bed. Next she gave a kiss to the middle brother. He was still sleeping in his green bed.

엄마는 파란 침대에서 평화롭게 자고 있는 가장 큰 형에게 가장 먼저 뽀뽀를 해주었어요. 그런 다음에 초록 침대에서 자고 있는 둘째 형에게 뽀뽀를 하였지요.

Finally, Mom went to Jimmy's orange bed, and gave him a kiss.

마지막으로, 엄마는 주황색 침대에서 자고 있는 지미에게 가서 뽀뽀를 해주었어요.

"Good morning, children," said Mom. "It's time to rise."

그리고 "얘들아, 아침이란다. 이제 일어나야지" 라고 엄마가 얘기했어요.

Getting out of bed, the oldest brother made his way to the bathroom.

가장 큰 형이 침대에서 일어나 화장실에 갔어요.

"Wow!" he shouted, "I have a brand-new toothbrush! It's blue, my favorite color. Thank you, Mom." He started to brush his teeth.

화장실에 간 형이 깜짝 놀라서 소리쳤어요, "우와! 새 칫솔이 있네요! 제가 좋아하는 파란색이에요. 고마워요, 엄마." 그리고 큰 형은 이를 닦기 시작했어요.

The middle brother followed him. "I have a new toothbrush as well, and mine's green!" he exclaimed and also began to brush his teeth.

그 말을 듣고 둘째 형이 화장실로 갔어요. 둘째 형도 깜짝 놀라서 소리쳤어요, "저도 새 칫솔이 있네요. 제 것은 초록색이에요!" 그리고 둘째 형도 이를 닦기 시작했어요.

Jimmy got out of bed and walked slowly towards the bathroom. *Why even bother brushing my teeth?* he thought. *My teeth are fine as they are.*

지미도 침대에서 일어나 천천히 화장실로 걸어 갔어요. 지미는 이렇게 생각했어요. 귀찮은데 이를 왜 닦아야 하지? 안 닦아도 괜찮은데.

"Look, Jimmy," said his oldest brother, "you have a new toothbrush too. It's orange like your bed."
지미가 화장실에 오자 큰 형이 얘기했어요. "지미야, 이거 봐봐. 너도 새 칫솔이 생겼어. 네 침대랑 똑같은 주황색이야."

"So I have a new toothbrush, big deal." Jimmy stood in front of the mirror, but he still didn't start brushing his teeth.
지미는 "새 칫솔 생긴 게 큰일도 아닌걸" 이라고 대답했어요. 그리고 거울 앞에 섰지만, 지미는 이 닦기를 시작하지 않았지요.

"Kids, hurry up! Breakfast is almost ready," they heard their mother's soft voice. "Has everyone finished brushing their teeth?"
엄마가 부드러운 목소리로 아이들을 불렀어요, "얘들아, 서두르렴! 아침 식사준비가 다 되어가고 있단다. 다들 이를 닦았지?"

"I've finished," answered the oldest brother and ran out of the bathroom.
"다 했어요." 라고 큰 형이 대답하고 화장실에서 나갔어요.

"Me too," replied the middle brother. He ran after his brother to the kitchen.
그리고 둘째 형도 "저도 다했어요." 라고 대답하고 부엌으로 갔어요.

"Mom, I finished brushing my teeth too," shouted Jimmy. He was just about to leave the bathroom, when he heard a voice.
"엄마, 저도 이를 닦았어요." 라고 지미가 소리쳤어요. 지미가 화장실에서 나가려고 하자 어떤 목소리가 들렸어요.

"It's not nice to lie," the voice said. "You didn't brush your teeth."
"거짓말은 나쁜 거야, 지미야. 너는 이를 닦지 않았잖아."

"Who said that?" asked Jimmy as he looked around in confusion.

"누구지?" 깜짝 놀란 지미는 주변을 돌아보았어요.

Frowning at him was his new orange toothbrush, standing on the counter. He just couldn't believe his eyes...or his ears!

그건 바로 세면대에 있는 주황색 칫솔이었죠. 지미는 눈으로 보고, 귀로 들어도 믿을 수가 없었어요!

"A toothbrush can't talk," he said in a stunned voice.

"칫솔이 말을 하다니 말도 안 돼", 지미는 떨리는 목소리로 말했어요.

"I sure can. I'm a magical toothbrush," said the toothbrush proudly. "My job is to make sure EVERYONE brushes his teeth."

"나는 마법의 칫솔이라서 말을 할 수가 있어. 그리고 모두가 이를 닦도록 하는 게 내 일이야" 라고 칫솔이 큰 소리로 말했어요.

Jimmy laughed in response. "I didn't brush my teeth and nothing bad happened to me."

지미가 웃으면서 대답했어요. "나는 이를 닦지 않아도 아무 문제가 없었어."

"Look at yourself," the brush said. "Your teeth are yellow and your breath smells terrible."
그러자 칫솔이 이야기했어요, "네 이를 좀 보렴. 이가 노랗고, 입 냄새도 나빠."

"That's not true, brush. You're just making it up!" Jimmy took the toothbrush and threw it far into the corner of the bathroom.
"말도 안 돼. 칫솔아, 너는 거짓말쟁이야!" 지미는 칫솔을 쥐고 화장실 끝에 던져버렸어요.

Then he ran into the kitchen to have his breakfast.
그리고 부엌으로 달려가서 밥을 먹었어요.

"That's no way to treat me," shouted the toothbrush. "I'm a magical toothbrush. I'll prove how important I am!"

"나를 이렇게 함부로 다루다니!" 칫솔이 소리치며 말했어요. "나는 마법의 칫솔이야. 내가 얼마나 중요한지 알려 줄거다!"

By this time, Jimmy was already sitting down next to his brothers in the kitchen.

지미는 부엌에서 형들의 옆에 앉아서 식사를 하는 중이었어요.

He took a sandwich and brought it to his mouth. But then the sandwich jumped out of Jimmy's hands right onto the plate of his oldest brother.

지미가 샌드위치를 한 입 물려고 하자 샌드위치가 갑자기 지미의 손에서 떨어져서 큰 형의 접시 위로 올라갔어요.

Instead of the sandwich, Jimmy had bitten his fingers — hard!

지미는 샌드위치 대신에 손가락을 깨물어 버렸어요- 정말 세게요!

"Who does this sandwich belong to?" the brother asked.

"이 샌드위치는 누구의 것이야?" 큰 형이 물었어요.

"My sandwich ran away from me," answered Jimmy. "It's mine!"

"내 샌드위치가 도망갔었어. 이것은 내 것이야!" 라고 지미가 대답했어요.

"Quite an imagination you have, sweetie. How can a sandwich run away?" his mother said.

"이제 상상은 그만하렴, 아가야. 샌드위치가 어떻게 도망을 가니?" 라고 엄마가 말했어요.

"I don't know how, but that's really what happened," said Jimmy.

"어떻게 도망간 건지는 저도 몰라요 하지만 정말이에요." 라고 지미가 말했어요.

Then, Mom gave him a big plate full of salad. "Here, perhaps you would like to eat a delicious vegetable salad instead," she said.

그러자 엄마가 샐러드로 가득찬 접시를 주었어요. "그러면 샌드위치 대신에 맛있는 야채를 먹는 것이 좋겠구나" 라고 엄마가 말했어요.

"Yummy, I love vegetable salad," said Jimmy, about to start eating. Suddenly, the salad plate leaped up and settled down on the table near his middle brother.

"맛있겠다. 샐러드는 정말 좋아요" 라고 지미가 말했어요. 지미가 한 입 먹으려고 하자, 갑자기 샐러드 그릇이 번쩍 뛰어서 둘째 형 자리로 옮겨갔어요.

"Look," said the middle brother, "how did your plate get over here?"

"어! 어떻게 그릇이 여기로 올 수 있지?" 라고 둘째 형이 말했어요.

"You were right, honey! Your food is running away from you!" said their astonished mom. "That's strange."

"음식이 지미에게서 도망가네! 정말 이상하구나" 라고 엄마가 놀란 목소리로 말했어요.

"Mom, I'm getting hungry already. What can I eat?" said Jimmy.

"엄마 배고파요. 어떻게 해야 먹을 수 있죠?" 라고 지미가 엄마에게 물었어요.

Mom thought for a moment. "How about your favorite carrot cake? I'll give you a big slice."

엄마는 잠시 생각하고 이야기했어요. "지미가 좋아하는 당근 케이크는 어떨까? 엄마가 큰 조각을 줄게."

"Oh yes, carrot cake! I love it so much," Jimmy shouted happily, "Thanks, Mom."

"당근 케이크는 정말 좋아요! 감사합니다, 엄마." 라고 지미가 행복한 목소리로 소리쳤어요.

However, before Jimmy could take the cake, it began float in the air. It flew into the living room and settled on the couch.

하지만 지미가 케이크를 받기도 전에, 케이크가 공중에 뜨기 시작했어요. 케이크는 거실을 날아 다니다가 소파에 정착했어요.

Jimmy hopped out of his chair and started chasing the piece of cake.

지미는 의자에서 껑충 내려와서 케이크를 쫓기 시작했어요.

He jumped on the sofa, but the cake zoomed back to the table. Jimmy ran back to the table and then the cake flew out of the house. Jimmy rushed after it.

지미가 소파에서 껑충 뛰었지만, 케이크는 식탁으로 휙 하고 날아갔어요. 지미는 다시 식탁으로 뛰어갔지만, 케이크는 집안 곳곳을 날아 다녔어요.

The cake looped around the house while Jimmy trailed behind it. Another round and another and another, and still Jimmy followed.

지미는 케이크를 뒤쫓고 케이크는 집안을 마구 돌아다녔어요. 지미는 계속 뛰었지만, 여전히 케이크를 잡지 못했어요.

Until he had run out of breath. Tired, Jimmy sat down at the entrance of the house and started crying.

지미는 숨이 찰 때까지 뛰다가 지쳐 버리자 집 앞의 현관에 앉아서 울기 시작했어요.

At the same moment, two of his friends were passing by. "Hey, Jimmy," they greeted. "Why are you sitting here looking so sad? Come play with us."

그때, 친구 두 명이 지나가면서 인사했어요. "지미야, 안녕! 왜 그렇게 슬픈 표정으로 앉아 있어? 우리랑 같이 놀자."

"Yes, I'd like that!" Jimmy ran towards them. "You won't believe what happened to me today!"

지미는 친구들을 보고 달려가며 얘기했어요. "그래, 좋아! 오늘 정말 신기한 일이 있었는데, 지금 말해 줄게!"

But, as he opened his mouth, the friends shouted,

하지만, 지미가 입을 열자 친구들이 소리쳤어요.

"Yikes, what a stink! We'll go play somewhere else while you go brush your teeth!" With that, they ran away.

"우웩, 기분 나쁜 냄새가 나네! 우리는 다른 데로 가서 놀게, 너는 이를 닦는 것이 좋겠다!" 친구들은 그렇게 말하고 지미에게서 도망쳤어요.

Bursting into tears yet again, Jimmy entered the house.
지미는 눈물을 터트리며 집에 들어 갔어요.

He went to the bathroom and saw the magical toothbrush flying in the air. "Hello, Jimmy. I've been waiting for you. Do you want to brush your teeth now?" Jimmy nodded.
지미가 화장실에 가자 하늘을 날아 다니는 마법의 칫솔이 미소를 지으며 이야기했어요, "안녕, 지미야. 너를 기다리고 있었어. 이제 이를 닦고 싶니?" 그러자 지미가 고개를 끄덕였어요.

Jimmy started brushing his teeth, from one side to the other, top and bottom, front and back. He brushed his teeth until they became white and shiny.
지미는 좌우, 위아래, 앞뒤로 이를 닦기 시작했어요. 하얗게 빛날 때까지 이를 닦았어요.

Gazing proudly at his reflection in the mirror, Jimmy said, "Thank you, brush. It was even nice and pleasant to brush my teeth. I now have sweet-smelling breath too."

지미는 거울에 비치는 자신을 자신있게 바라보면서 말했어요, "고마워, 칫솔아. 이를 닦는 것은 정말 멋지고 즐거운 일이야. 이제 입 냄새도 좋아졌어."

"You look great," said the brush. "By the way, my name is Leah. I'm always here to help."

"지미야, 이제 네 이가 좋아보여. 아 그리고, 내 이름은 레아야. 내가 항상 이를 닦는 것을 도와줄게." 라고 칫솔이 말했어요.

That's how Jimmy and Leah became good friends. Ever since that day, they've seen each other twice a day to protect Jimmy's teeth and help them grow strong and healthy.

그날 이후로, 지미의 이가 강하고 건강해지도록, 지미와 레아는 하루에 두 번씩 보는 좋은 친구가 되었답니다.

Made in the USA
Lexington, KY
26 May 2017